strong female protagonist

poems by

Heather M. Hoover

Finishing Line Press
Georgetown, Kentucky

strong female protagonist

ACKNOWLEDGMENTS

"Teaching Literature" appeared in the Snapdragon Journal
Four poems appeared in my chapbook, *If Moon, Then Yes* (Dancing Girl
Press, 2018): "Lost Lyric" (revised in this volume); "Girl Before a Mirror;"
"Family Portrait;" "Suppose"

As ever, I am grateful to Randy, for his love and support, and to my children,
Owen and Violet who inspire me every day. Many thanks to my Papaw, who
encouraged my first love of poetry, to my Uncle Shelly for keeping my hands
full of books, and to my mother, who read to me.

And thank you to all the amazing women in my life, especially Amy
Edmonds, Becky Kenworthy, Cara Beth Brackins, Kayla Walker Edin,
Shauna Nefos Webb, Miriam Perkins, and Heather Armstrong (who is also
to be thanked for the cover art)—real-life strong female protagonists all.

Finally, thank you to my daughter Violet to whom this volume is dedicated.
She recently proposed a new improv club at her middle school, in part
because she observed, "it's as important to know when to change the story as
it is to keep it going." I have a lot to learn from her.

Publisher: Leah Huete de Maines
Editor: Christen Kincaid
Cover Art: Heather K. Armstrong
Author Photo: Randy W. Hoover
Cover Design: Elizabeth Maines McCleavy

Order online: www.finishinglinepress.com
also available on amazon.com

Author inquiries and mail orders:
Finishing Line Press
PO Box 1626
Georgetown, Kentucky 40324
USA

Contents

For Violet

Monday

In the freshly painted
windowsill
where the morning light
falls soft and easy

a cicada-killer wasp
rests upside down
in the gap between
sill and screen.

her stinger curves
over the edge,
elegant sliver
spiked with venom.

gingerly, I retrieve her
perfectly preserved body

bowed with intent,
antennae alert
dirt still clinging
to her shapely legs

her glossy black and yellow abdomen,
like some soak-stain modernist
painting, narrows
to an impossibly
tiny waist

her lightly-fuzzed thorax
braces translucent amber
wings, veined
and delicate, delicate;

did her blood throb there,
heart pumping wildly
through the single blood
vessel to her head

as she struggled
fruitlessly to burrow
into the metal screen?

Even in death, her head
bends toward her task
unseeing,

those unbearably lovely
antennae attuned
to the wrong channel

an instinct for survival
that let her down
instead of bidding her
look up.

Red Sky in Mourning

The sky oranges and pinks
on my drive to work
and i'm seized
by the urge to pull
to the side of the road,
snap a picture i know
will not capture
the intensity of what
these colors make me feel—
the arc of ache—is it cruel
to want to share it, not the way
i know it will be posted
to every feed in a matter of hours
preserving it for those unlucky
enough to sleep through the riot,
but
i think of calling my mother
of the long silence between us
to talk of hurt and forgiveness
i imagine scream-singing
the folksy song pulsing in the background
or burying my face in my newborn's
chubby neck, an impossible 15-year
journey to the past
i want to cry, but no tears come
so i keep driving forward
to my destination
watch from a parking lot
where the beautiful sky-wound
drips and oozes into my
travel mug of lukewarm coffee
thinking all the while
how the view might be better
from the top of the mountain
or the nearby steeple
or if all these damn power lines
disappeared   in the end,

i don't even take a picture
i don't do anything
but sit in my overly-warm car
out of place and time.

Remember

The octopus, reeling
as a blind brute
shark swims away
with her arm,
blanches, retreats feebly
to her den.

She does not eat,
she does not hunt,
she does not play.

She only breathes in
and breathes out.

Wrapped tightly
in her remaining limbs,
she concentrates
on becoming
whole, even though

her life is short,
and she could make
do with only seven.

Until at last,
she emerges, tiny
perfect arm curled
against her own
amazing body.

Thanksgiving

waking up
to news of another
shooting, today's
standard fare,
but a feast laid
years ago—

pies fluted with
grief, table laden
with the old story
of bullets planted
generations past
by men greedy
for more
abundant crops

who nurtured tender
shoots with rage
and righteousness
afraid of losing what
they already imagined
they owned

and the yield
so ample,
that we set aside
a day to commemorate,
to choke down
extra helpings
casings and all,

wounds dressed
with gravy
and myth.

When the Apocalypse Comes

when the apocalypse comes, what will you put into the vessel for
the future?
Ocean Vuong

not the axe at my roots,
or the battle plans

not the flag whiting
out the horizon

not this book of creeds
tooth-bared, claw-sharpened

not this language of death
or this box of grief

not this uniform image
unrefracted.

when the waters come,
it will be this throbbing,
twined cord,
these heartmouth words,
the starshine of our hands
interlaced
stories sieving sorrow

it will be this soil,
humming with conversation
we could not hear before

seeding some new, vibrating
song gently
into this body.

Friday, 3:17 p.m. Pandemic Time

The Crow Bar's neon
sign flashes

open

open

to an empty parking lot
on the forgotten side
of town.

I imagine the barkeep inside,
arranging, rearranging
glassware

noticing a jagged gash
in the vinyl stool,

watching television
prophets forecast
doom
from their honored
perch in the corner
above the billiards table,

killing time,
waiting for this
shift to end.

Au Revoir Rêve

At a certain age
you realize
that you might never
learn French.

And the vague
dream of Paris:
writing in cafes
with the ghost
of Gertrude Stein
becomes another kind
of ghost

tucked between the pages
of a journal.

Receipt

The horehound
sitting on a shelf
of old-timey candies

speaks in her voice,
the lilting drawl
flattened by years
in the Midwest.

She asks what
I am cooking tonight
with this cart full
of glossy vegetables
and brown paper packages
of meat

I gather her
into the basket,
wind my way through
fluorescent aisles
listening to her stories,
feeding her news
of these many years past.

Later, in my kitchen,
I tell her about the carrots,
the potatoes, the onions,
the soft red cubes of beef,
the hot oil shining
in the dutch oven, anticipating
company
the wine bubbling (*we
used beer*, she says.)
I remember this
(*don't forget the bay leaf*)
I bring the jar to my nose,
catching the Christmasy scent

Salt in the well of my palm
is the right amount—
and time, longer
than a person might realize

until it is stew steaming
in white bowls
on the table.

Her voice, stronger now,
I remember this.

Raising the spoon to my lips,
I remember you.

Family Portrait

The picture of the four of us
in front of a new house,
not faded, but unmistakably
another time.

Four smiles, linked by inside
jokes, knowing glances, dinners
gathered around a cheap,
glass-topped table: first steps,
layoffs, squeezed paychecks
and piano lessons.

Those four people—gone,
the neighborhood no longer
desirable.
The house must still be there,
though, and I wonder on occasion
who lives there now.

Lost Lyric

> *Once Cretan girls used to dance*
> *harmoniously like this,*
> *soft-footed about the fair*
> *altar...*
> *They made for the tender grass.*
> —*Sappho's fragment 16*

In her best stories
she drank
blackberry wine
and danced
full of music
and summertime

tiny waist
high cheekbones
sharp eyes
so say the faded Polaroids with her
lilting scrawl: *summer picnic, at the races*

I did not know her to
be a dancer,
rocking in her
chair by the door,
house sealed against
the heat,
the cold;
her feet gnarled
with bunions,
her legs stiff,

having strayed
so far
so long
from tender grass.

Banana Bread

The last two bananas
browned overnight
on the counter

their freckled, too-
sweet flesh courting
ripe and rot.

I cannot bear
to eat them—
nor can I bear
to bury them
in the depths
of the kitchen
garbage.

Far away, some
fungus munches
acres of groves

lack of diversity,
scientists say.
Inevitable,
scientists say.

Powerless
to halt the onset
of certain destruction,
I have only

flour and sugar,
egg and oil
to sublimate death
into promise
to coax
loaf from loss.

Bounty

Something is eating
the bean plants;

cabbage moths
destroyed the cauliflower;

worms raided the lettuce,
beetles claimed the potatoes;

the first of two zucchinis
sampled and left to rot—

with each failure,
laden jars disappear
from cellar storage,
forkfuls evaporate
into imagination.

A rabbit, ears-pricked
for danger
bounds from the carrots
feinting only
to garden's edge,
knowing;

and where the glossy sweet potato leaves
undulate in the thick
summer air, a groundhog
raises his head,
loping away unhurried,
full and fat.

Whale Song

Far from shore
two whales
leap and frolic
in the morning sunshine,

their bulk, momentarily
weightless between sky
and ocean;

hours later we wade
timidly into the waves,
our own bodies fragile,
not made for swimming

plunging finally
under the cold water
where their melodious banter
envelops us
and we surface, wide-eyed
holding our breath,
diving again and again
beneath the surface

even though they do not
sing for us.

Prayer

a single dust mote
gliding illuminated

on this morning sun
arcing over pine boards.

once perhaps part
of some distant star

witness
to depth and dark

falling through
the shaft of light.

Eight

Eight is curious
but not self-conscious
independent but
still naïve
eight tells stories
that don't make sense
and surprises us with jokes
that land,
timing perfect.

Eight is golden-haired
and new glasses,
eight is helpful, kind,
sometimes underfoot,
sings in the shower,
hums unconsciously,
music flowing from her,
and sunshine,
her lungs tiny and strong
her bones still growing

her tilted head
in complete
credulity;
premonition
and possibility.

Improvisation

My young daughter
  has abandoned
her scales
  to range the keyboard
arpeggiating, coaxing
  harmonies from keys
she cannot read
  on the page
her small body
  bent in concentration
head bowed toward
  some inner music
mournful, ancient

All the while,
  families huddle
in a subway station
  listening to explosions
thunder above ground
  laying waste
a once-beautiful city.
  An ordinary life
rendered criminal
  by camo-clad soldiers
following orders,
conjuring enemies
of mothers, teachers, priests.

Her music crests,
  crescendos, staccato
bass pulsing,
  propelling her toward
a nearly miraculous
  final sequence.
How could she know,

how does she hear
this impossible chord
    suspended
like grief
        between possibilities?

Daffodils

By late June
the daffodils
with their jolly
yellow megaphones

have retreated underground—
slim, green shoots
all that remains of their
heraldic primary color

their slow departure
escaped my notice
distracted as I was
by the usual culprits.

many years ago,
thousands, it seems,
my young son clutched
the *daffodilder's* sturdy stems
in his tiny fingers,
his blue eyes earnest
with the gravity of this gift

and year after year,
we oohed and ahhed
his lopsided bouquets
on the kitchen counter,
those sweet daffodilder bunches

until inevitably, that extra syllable
too slipped quietly away
undetected until the season passed

while still-deep roots
prepare a song
of new beginnings
unseen in the dark.

Antiphony

Just before the sun disappears
below the mountains,

a cardinal lights
in the tulip magnolia

red flame against soft pink
cheek of blossom

his song insistent,
repetitive, unhurried

the last note shared
with some unseen partner

recapitulating
but for a flourish at the end—

call and response
into the hastening night.

the same singers, perhaps,
who herald the sun's rising
confident even
in the 4 a.m. dark.

Ruby-throated hummingbird

Poised in midair,
her tiny green body
hovers over the white
soapwort blossom,
wings beating invisibly.

She pauses,
drinking deeply
from each flower.

She masters stillness
for a moment,
moving and not moving.

She lingers
for only one of my heartbeats,
but hundreds
of her own.

Suppose

you were a field mouse
with only so many
allotted heart beats

would you breathe deeper
move slower
or would you forge ahead
lining a nest for winter's chill

Considering Picasso's "Girl Before a Mirror"

Time
reduced to lines
and shapes
no less
haunted

Teaching Literature

Suits demand market value,
equivalencies, and progress
reports that cannot
contain this fluttering

vibrant pulse crackling
an invitation
to inhabit another skin,
another time

or this one, fully

like the electron exchange
of human touch, never
finished or absolute
but vulnerably becoming
a space

for unknowing
discovery (its verb,
transitive,
from the French
to disclose oneself).

The foot taps impatiently,
expensive, leather-sheathed
against etymologies:

How much is it worth

and this wrong question
buzzards
over the spines worth
nothing, everything.

Ars Poetica

Dickinson imagined
the top of her head
taken off—

by which, did she mean
clarity or ecstasy,
her scalp peeled away
leaving only white, gleaming
bone and gray matter

that place where the tips
of my fingers rest
when the words
sneak in and out?

Michelangelo, the guide says,
coaxed David's body from a block
of flawed marble, working
without food or sleep,
chiseling through downpours

polishing each vein,
attending to ligaments,
striations of muscle,
the jugular pulse,

feverishly freeing
the body he knew
to be hidden
in the block.

strong female protagonist

the old man, smelling of boardrooms with leatherette swivel chairs and Arthurian round tables
glances at my pithy t-shirt, worn for emphasis in a lecture on feminism;
his eyes linger too long on the "o" and the "i," his thin lips glistening as he tongues
the words, like a child sounding out his first story: *what is a strong female protagonist?*
his breath stinking of stale coffee, his hand uninvited on my shoulder, attention already drifting
when I reach behind his ear and pluck out a gleaming silver sword, curved and elegant;
his eyes roll in confusion as I march him through the door,
the one reserved for a certain kind of meetings, the one whose door is usually closed,
my sword at his throat until he breaks for the corner, sputtering with fury before I run the table
slicing it into tiny slivers of wood with precision, whittling them into tiny dagger-like pencils
swirling the scraps into pulp until they parch, papering the room, the floor, the old man
who has receded into the background of my rhythm:
I am. I am. I am.

Heather M. Hoover has been teaching strong literary female protagonists for over twenty years. This collection chronicles her attempts learn from and emulate those courageous women characters and authors, but it also looks to her grandmother, her mother, and her daughter for inspiration. She considers the lives they have lived, the choices they made, and the potential to make new ones. Hoover earned a Ph.D. from UT Knoxville, and she teaches literature, humanities, and writing at a small liberal arts college in East Tennessee. She is the author of *Composition as Conversation: Seven Virtues for Effective Writing*, and has published poems in *Leaven, Snapdragon,* and in *The Southern Poetry Anthology* Tennessee Volume. Her chapbook *If Moon, Then Yes,* was published by Dancing Girl Press in 2018. She lives in Johnson City, TN with her family.

www.ingramcontent.com/pod-product-compliance
Lightning Source LLC
Chambersburg PA
CBHW022058080426
42734CB00009B/1399